TITLE PAGE

Real Estate Agent

Real Estate Agent Bible

Ebuka Ugboma

COPYRIGHT

©Ebuka Ugboma 2022

DISCLAIMER

This book is not intended to replace expert advice.

Table of Content

Dedication

This Book is dedicated to my lovely Mom

Acknowledgement

Special thanks to God Almighty. The ultimate giver of knowledge and wisdom

ABOUT THE AUTHOR

Gary Austine Ebuka Ugboma Esq FICMC, ACIArb UK, FMA, AGIS, PMP

LLB Hons, BA Hons, Dip Mus Ed, Pdip Bus Admin, PDip Estate Mgt, MBA, MSC Peace and conflict resolution.

Ebuka Ugboma has multiple degrees from different Universities across different fields; Arts, Law, Social Sciences and Humanities generally. He is a Chartered Arbitrator and Mediator, trained in the style and pattern of Chartered Institute Of Arbitrators UK.

Ebuka Ugboma has successfully published many books including Propensities And Habits For Success

Check out and buy his books on Amazon:

https://www.amazon.com/Ebuka-Ugboma/e/B0B6HHVVW6

Email: garyugboma@gmail.com Phone: 2348033924157

Chapter 1

INTRODUCTION

Real Estate has always been a lucrative industry. It is estimated that the Real Estate industry will reach a trillion dollars in a few years. This is why Real Estate Agencies are so valuable. With an Agency, you will be able to reach a wide range of people, from first-time buyers to potential investors, to affordably rent or purchase a home. In this book, I will give you a few tips on how to get started in the Real Estate industry, how Agents make money, and how to find a successful Agency.

What Is A Real Estate Agency?

A Real Estate Agency is a company or an organization that is authorized by the government to represent sellers and buyers of Real Estate. The Agency also acts as a liaison between the two parties. The Agency often has a team of people who help them find clients and sell properties. For example, they would search for properties that are on sale, evaluate whether or not this property is suitable for their buyers, and tell the seller if the price of the house has to be adjusted.

This is what makes an authentic Real Estate Agency stand out. If it is an honest and legitimate Agency, then it will be able to help you find a property that suits your needs. It is also more capable of helping you negotiate the price of the home and making sure everything is legal.

Chapter 2

How To Get Started as a Real Agent?

It's a question that more and more people are asking themselves: "How do I get started as a Real Estate Agent?" But before you can start earning money as a Real Estate Agent, you need to know the basics.

This post will help you learn how to get started as a Real Estate Agent with everything from industry knowledge and skills that Agents need, working in the field of Real Estate, local regulations and licensing requirements, profiles of successful Agents who have built their careers on these very things, advice on what types of companies are best for emerging brokers who want to start out their career immediately.

And remember — the more you learn about Real Estate, and the more you develop your experience and skill set, the better prepared you'll be before submitting your license application and passing your state's licensing exam.

How To Get Started As A Real Estate Agent

#1: Take A Course!

Imagine this… You've just graduated college and are ready to dive into your first career (and hopefully, earn some money). You attend college for four years, learn a bunch of stuff about the world, graduate with honors and you can't wait to get started.

But should you go right out and start working on your Real Estate license? Of course not! You want to be smart when it comes to career decisions, so the first thing you need to do is get some professional education.

You know what they say: a little bit of knowledge is a dangerous thing because it could become a whole lot more than that if you're not careful…

You have many options when it comes to taking courses in Real Estate. In such courses you can learn Real Estate law, Real Estate finance, as well as about marketing and selling Real Estate.

For example, some colleges offer a certificate program in Real Estate. Others require you to take several classes in succession to earn a degree. Then there are also training schools that offer classes for people seeking a career in selling property.

Whatever it is that you want to study and accomplish on your educational journey, make sure that the school is accredited by the appropriate state Agency. And make sure to check out its reputation among consumers and current students alike before applying for the course(s).

#2: Practice, Practice, Practice!

There's an old saying that says, "Practice makes perfect." And we think it applies perfectly to Real Estate. Just as athletes practice their craft and artists practice their skills, Real Estate Agents must continue to hone their skills beyond the classroom and into the field to get better and better at what they do.

While studying in school is important, it's also important that you get out into the field and practice your new-found knowledge. You'll learn more in two weeks of on-the-job training than you will from a month of training in a classroom…

That's why many Real Estate schools have internship programs available for students looking to get a jump start on beginning a career in selling property. These programs can provide you with a ton of experience, especially when it comes to understanding the processes and protocols that Real Estate professionals follow every day.

If you're thinking about getting into a Real Estate course or considering taking an internship program, let's talk about what you need to know first. Continue reading below to learn more!

#3: Work For A Real Estate Company

No matter how difficult it is for a Real Estate Agent to get established, it's even more difficult for them to break into the field. And that's why many aspiring Real Estate Agents choose to work for a large company in their area before going out on their own and finding an Agency that they can operate:

Advantages of working in a large company Real Estate companies are usually good at providing training programs where you can polish your skills and develop a solid foundation. They also often have the resources needed to provide administrative support such as accounting and marketing. On top of all this, you may find opportunities within corporations where you can acquire extensive experience and further develop your professional network.

The "disadvantages" of working in a large corporation Typically, entry-level positions are restricted to administrative tasks and do not usually carry a large salary. Employee retention is often inconsistent and you may not have a lot of opportunity to develop professionally within the company.

#4: Find An Agency That You Can Work For!

If you've done your research, you know that there are many different types of Real Estate companies out there. Some are more established than others while some have better reputations than others. Some have only one office location while others may have multiple offices located all over the place.

Chapter 3

How do Real Estate Agents make money?

Once you've found your Real Estate Agency, you may wonder how it is possible that they are in business. They have a team of Agents and office staff, so how can they still make money? The answer is that the Real Estate Agent only gets a small cut of the property it sells. The rest goes to the seller, who has sold their home or property. For example, if an Agent sells a house for $100 million dollars, then the Agency will get about $2 million dollars as their cut.

Real Estate Agents are paid on commission. This means that the more property they sell, the more money they make. However, the property has to be sold at full value – so the Agency has to ensure that their clients are getting a fair price.

The Real Estate Agent also helps Property owners to rent out their properties. This is also a way for the Real Estate Agent to make money – although not as much as if they sold the property.

However, it is still a source of income for them and an important part of their business.

Facility management is another way Real Estate Agents make money by providing apartments for people to live in. These complexes are often built and owned by Real Estate Agencies and so they can charge their tenants to live there. This fee then goes directly into their bank account. Sometimes an Agency can make more money from renting out these buildings than from property sales!

Real Estate Agents do Property flipping. This is where they buy a property, renovate it and then sell it on to the next buyer. This means that the Real Estate Agent has partnered with the contractor who is doing the renovations. They can then get together after selling the property to make more profit from selling onwards.

This practice is also legal in other countries as well – such as Hong Kong, Japan and China!

The Real Estate Agent also gets money from selling advertising space on their websites and brokerages. Services like "Property Search" are where any property advertiser can go to post their house for rent or sale, to be seen by all the other Real Estate

Agents in their area. All the Real Estate Agents have to do is pay a small fee for each property that they are promoting.

Real Estate Agents also collect money from their clients. They can take payments based on their percentage of the sale price, or in cash and then pay them later on when they hand the money over to the owner of the property. This can be good for both people, who want to pay in full, and Property Owners who want cash now. The Real Estate Agent can get a fee from both of these transactions, as they are the middle-person.

Chapter 4

How can I find a Real Estate company?

Another way of finding a Real Estate Agent is to learn about others and read reviews online. If you don't want to spend your time searching for an Agency, then you can always use your social media accounts and search for Real Estate agencies in your area. You can also use online websites to find an Agency.

Once you've found a good Real Estate Agency, you can start your search for a property. When searching online, make sure to know the market and neighbourhood so that you don't drive past a million houses in the wrong area. You want to find a home with potential and potential value – so make sure to look for homes that are in good neighbourhoods and affordable.

How Can I Find Out If An Agent Is Successful?

One way of finding out if an Agent is successful is by studying their website. Make sure to read over the website carefully. Is it professional? Are the photos of their properties good? Do they have testimonials and reviews from satisfied clients?

Another way of learning if an Agent is successful is by talking to the Agent. You can start off by asking them about their reputation and whether or not they have had a lot of success with their clients. Find out if they have a lot of customers and if they are able to close deals successfully.

Chapter 5

What are the best types of Real Estate agencies?

The best Real Estate agencies will give you ways to get started in the industry without having to pay for training courses or certification tests.

What Do I Need For My Real Estate Business?

As we've said before, you have to have a plan before starting anything. With Real Estate, you have to have a plan of attack. With this in mind, let's go through a few things you will need for your Real Estate business:

1. A Real Estate license

To sell and buy property legally, you will need a Real Estate license. This shows that the government trusts your ability to represent potential buyers and sellers of property. Your license will tell everyone else that you know what you are doing. You can find information on getting your license by going online or going directly to the Agency where you want to work.

2. The ability to sell

In order to be a Real Estate Agent, you must be able to sell and buy property. This will mean that you must have knowledge of the market and the neighbourhood. You can't just take anyone off the street and tell them that they are buying a house. The best way is to find out what people in your area want before you decide which properties are for sale and which ones aren't. Once you have the information, show it to people who will be interested in it but can't afford it right now. You can also give an honest appraisal if they ask for it.

3. A good network and experience

Your network is your credibility. You can't just go to the market and start selling and buying houses. That will not only help you in a very small way, but it will also affect your reputation. If you are seen as someone who is too desperate to buy or sell a house, then that will not only lower your price, but it may also hurt the confidence of potential buyers in your Agency. Instead, find out from others how they started their Real Estate business. Chances are that they had access to other people who could help them get started in the industry.

4. A knowledge of the market and neighbourhood

As we've already said, you can't just drive around and look for houses that are for sale. You have to have a good idea of what is happening in your area. Once again, this is best done online as well as with publications and data provided by Real Estate Agents in the area.

Chapter 6

How Much Do Real Estate Agents Make?

The amount of money you will make is going to depend on a number of factors. The first thing that you'll need to know about is how much people typically pay for homes in your area. The answer to that is going to be different for each Agent. What we can tell you is the average amount of home buyers pay for a house in your area. You need to understand that if your client is paying around $1.5 million dollars, then you will be getting a percentage of that.

If you want to work as an Agent, then you'll need at least 200 homes sold per year. If you do this, then over the course of two years, you will net about $25 million in profit. Again, these numbers are based on averages – so your results may be different. However, if you want to make the most out of this career choice, then you will want to put in the work necessary to get these results.

There are also a number of different ways that Real Estate Agents can make money in addition to their cut of commissions and fees. For instance, they can choose to buy properties and sell them later in order to create a profit margin. They may also have access to a mortgage company and be able to lend money towards houses as well as buying them at a lower rate and resell them at a higher one.

Real Estate Agents and their business partners also have the option of going on to start their own agencies. With this, they can build up a reputation amongst Real Estate Agents in the area and be placed on a pedestal. This is the dream of many Real Estate Agents and it is your right to aim for it as well.

Chapter 7

Safety tips for Real Estate Agents

The first thing that you will need to do when you are starting out in a new area or entering a new business is study your surroundings. This means that you'll need to know what potential threats will come from your work as an Agent and how you can avoid them.

This is something that you have to do whenever you start a new business. You shouldn't just wait and see if there are dangers in the area. Instead, it is your job to know what they are before they even show up. If you don't, then there is a chance that someone will hurt you or your family with no reason as to why.

Pay Attention To:

1. Know the neighbourhood

Try to be as familiar with the area as possible. This will not only give you a better chance at selling or buying properties, but it will also keep you

on your guard. This is especially important if you're going to be driving
around late at night looking at the houses that are up for sale. While
there is nothing wrong with spending time in this neighbourhood, you
do need to be careful since there may be people who are actually
looking for a Real Estate Agent like yourself and know what they're
doing.

2. Know the people in your area

Being familiar with the people in your area is important even if you are
familiar with the area. This will give you a better idea of who lives
around you and what they do for a living. It is also going to allow you to
put faces on names and know what people are doing at all times.

3. Wait until it's light out

While there is nothing wrong with showing up to look at a house at
night, there is also nothing wrong with waiting until it's light out. If
there are any problems that come up, then you can call someone and
handle it before anything happens.

4. Be alert for red flags

If you're in an area where there have been crimes or property
problems, then you should be suspicious of the people. Sometimes this
will be obvious, but sometimes people will try to hide their behaviour or

try to act as if nothing happened. This is why it is so important to pay attention and know what is going on in the area.

5. **Bring a friend**

One of your best friends would not only give you a good laugh, but they would also keep you safe since they could help you keep an eye out for threats as well as help you handle threats that come your way.

Chapter 8

Tips For Getting Started

The following are some of the things that will help you get started in Real Estate.

1. Find a mentor – one of the best ways to get started is by finding someone who can give you pointers and knowledge as well as help you get your feet wet. Every business has them, so why shouldn't Real Estate be no different?

2. Networking – networking is something that will make all the difference in your success or failure in the industry. Start by making connections with all types of professionals, including contractors, plumbers and electricians as well as web designers and software developers. The more kinds of people you know and the more kinds of businesses you can offer them, the better.

3. Learn all about the Town – if you live in a Town, then you should learn all about it since that could be considered beneficial for your

career. You don't want to lose any opportunities because of ignorance or a lack of knowledge.

4. Educate yourself – this is a business that requires education so you must take time to learn everything that there is to know about it. This will help not only when you're working on deals, but also when it comes to marketing yourself as well as your business. You must make a good impression because you never know who will come along and how much your business will be worth in the future.

5. Be curious – this may sound strange, but this is a very important trait to have as you are starting your new business. Curiosity is going to help you learn new things and it will also help you learn how to figure things out when they aren't made clear. You can never know enough about the industry, so neither must you or your staff.

If you think that Real Estate Agents may have no problems finding customers and clients, then think again. This is a business where you have to be able to sell yourself as well as your services to the public. However, if you are able to accomplish this, then there is a great chance that you'll be able to build up your business into something great.

But never forget that when it comes to starting up a business, the two most important things that you will need are time and money. These two commodities are universal and you can use them in any type of business that you decide to start. However, it is also true that some businesses require more of one than others or may give back more than others depending on what they do.

It is also important that you do not try to do everything at once. This will only lead to a huge amount of stress and that can lead to problems as well as a business that is understaffed. The best thing you can do is to start with one aspect of your business and work on it until you are able to make it a success then move on to something else or add more things.

This may sound intimidating, but if you know what you're doing, then there is no reason why this won't work for you. As long as you make sure to plan everything out and you have a little bit of luck on your side, then you should be able to make a success of your business.

The next thing that you will want to do is start networking. It is important for everyone who's starting up any type of business to know or know someone who's in the business, especially if it's related to the one that you are going into. This is going to give you a leg up when it comes to getting started and even staying afloat along the way.

The best way to get started is by simply asking people if they know someone else who can give you some tips. This is a great way to make connections and it will allow you to develop a network where you can ask questions or receive answers when you need them.

When it comes down to getting started, this is the most important part of making it work for you. But if you follow these steps, then there is no reason why your business isn't going to be a success.

Conclusion

Thank you again for purchasing this book! I hope I was able to help you out.

The next step is to take the information that you have learned and put it into action. You want to put into practice what you have read in this book so that you can be successful in Real Estate investing.

Don't be afraid of taking a chance on yourself and use everything that you've learned from this book as a way to create a better life for yourself. If you do, then there's no telling where your business will end up.

The next step is to get into action and get started. Once you're in, then everything will fall into place. Be prepared for the future and be rational about what you're doing.

Remember, don't get too crazy trying to make money in Real Estate while you're a beginner. In order to succeed in Real Estate investing, you will need a long-term plan and the ability to stick with it. It can be easy to get distracted by the idea of making a lot of money fast, but if you do that then there is no telling how successful your business will be.

In order for you to build something that lasts, then you have to start out slow and build up to something that can last for many years. Be prepared for the long haul and be willing to put up with the "hiccups" along the way, since they will happen. The only way to deal with them is to take care of them as soon as you realize that they are happening.

Embrace the uncertainty. Don't be afraid of failing, because failing is going to be a part of your plan for success. Failures are a part of success and if you put enough things into action, then you will eventually be successful in whatever it is that you are trying to achieve.

I hope this guide has helped you start off on your journey toward becoming a Real Estate investor in no time. Take everything that you've learned from this book and use it to its fullest potential.

www.ingramcontent.com/pod-product-compliance
Lightning Source LLC
Chambersburg PA
CBHW070616160726
48003CB00005B/2311